History of the World

The U.S. Constitution

Don Nardo

KidHaven Press

KidHaven Press, an imprint of Gale Group, Inc.
P.O. Box 289009, San Diego, CA 92198-9009

Library of Congress Cataloging-in-Publication Data

Nardo, Don, 1947–
  The U.S. Constitution / by Don Nardo.
    p. cm. — (History of the world)
  Includes bibliographical references and index.
  ISBN 0-7377-0776-3 (alk. paper)
  Summary: Discusses the development and ratification of the
U.S. Constitution and the Bill of Rights and their influence
around the world.
    1. Constitutional law—United States—Juvenile literature.
  2. Constitutional history—United States—Juvenile literature.
  [1. Constitutional law—United States. 2. Constitutional history—
  United States. 3. United States—Politics and government.]
  I. Title: U.S. Constitution. II. Title.
    KF4550 .Z9 N37 2002
    342.73'02—dc21

                                              2001002342

Printed in the U.S.A.

Contents

Chapter  One

The Founders Draft the Constitution

The United States Constitution is one of the most important and famous documents in the world. First, it is the blueprint of the nation's government. In a series of statements called articles, it spells out exactly how that government is supposed to work. It describes the government's three basic branches—the **executive** (the president), **legislative** (the Congress), and **judiciary** (the Supreme Court). Various articles lay out the powers these branches have and the rules they must follow. Other articles tell the precise manner in which the people can elect their public officials.

The Constitution is also the cornerstone of American democracy. Without it, Americans would have no guarantee for the many freedoms they enjoy. People sometimes take these rights for granted. But just imagine if one could not worship the way one wanted. Or if the government kept people from expressing their personal opinions. Or if someone accused of a crime could not receive a fair trial. The part of the Constitution that safeguards these and

An original copy of the U.S. Constitution, with the signatures of its framers clearly visible at lower right.

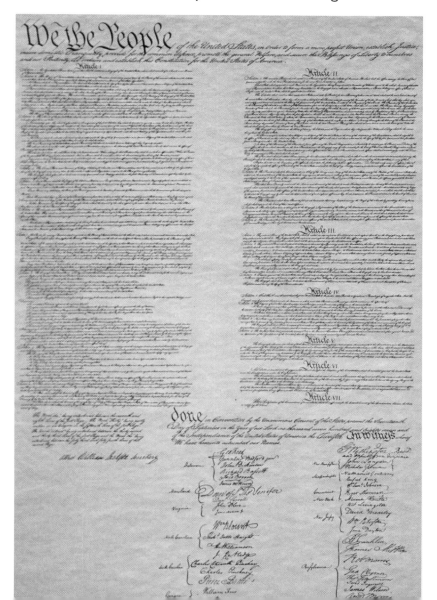

other basic human freedoms is called the Bill of Rights.

Protest and Revolution

The Europeans who first settled the area now occupied by the United States could *not* take such freedoms for granted. They came from various European nations where kings ruled. The settlers were still citizens of these nations, which they viewed as their "mother countries." So the colonies the settlers created in America followed the customs and laws of those mother countries. A country's king could change the laws and restrict freedom in the colonies at any time. And the colonists had no choice but to obey.

Such was the case with Great Britain and its North American colonies. By the early 1700s, the British had thirteen of them, stretching north to south along the Atlantic coast. At first the colonists were content to be British citizens. They felt that Britain had some of the fairest laws and most generous freedoms in all of Europe.

But in the 1760s, Britain's king and legislature, called Parliament, began imposing new taxes and laws on the American colonies. Seeing these as unfair, the colonists protested. And when the protests failed, they declared their independence from Britain. In 1776 the Revolution's leaders, today often called the founders, announced the birth of a new nation—the United States of America. Britain, however, was not willing

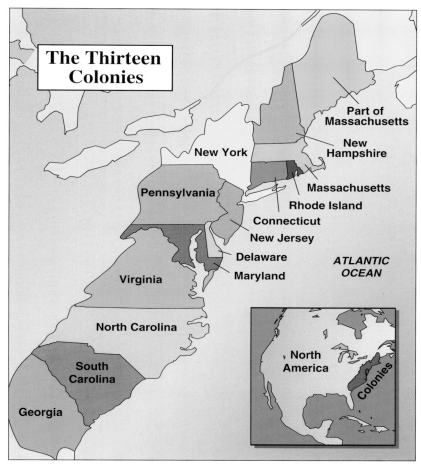

The Thirteen Colonies

Part of Massachusetts

New Hampshire

New York

Massachusetts

Pennsylvania

Rhode Island

Connecticut

New Jersey

Delaware

ATLANTIC OCEAN

Virginia

Maryland

North Carolina

North America

Colonies

South Carolina

Georgia

to let go of its American colonies without a fight. It sent troops to stop the uprising. And the bloody conflict known as the Revolutionary War followed.

A Temporary Set of Laws and Rules

The Americans won the war in 1783. They were free at last from laws and taxes imposed by a faraway land. But with that freedom came a serious duty. The former colonists now had to decide what kind of government would be best for their new nation.

When Americans protested British taxes and other policies, the British responded with force. During the Boston Massacre, in March 1770, British soldiers fired into a crowd of American colonists.

In March 1781, while the war was still raging, American leaders had established a temporary set of laws and rules. It was known as the Articles of Confederation. The Articles of Confederation proved weak and ineffective in several ways. First and foremost, they did not provide for a chief executive. Congress created new policies and laws. But it had to assign some of its own members to carry them out, a process that turned out to be too disorderly and slow. One founder, Thomas Jefferson, complained:

"The smallest trifle [detail] occupies Congress as long as the most important action of legislation. The most important propositions [proposals] hang over from week to week and month to month [and] the thing is never done."[1] Most of Jefferson's colleagues agreed with him that the government needed a chief executive to make it run more smoothly.

The Articles of Confederation had other weaknesses, as well. For example, no person had to obey a law made by Congress unless his or her state chose to enforce it. That made the **federal**, or national, government weaker than the individual states. Clearly, it would be fairer and more effective if everyone in the country had to follow the same rules.

Thomas Jefferson, seen here in a portrait by Gilbert Stuart, argued that the country needed a chief executive.

The Constitutional Convention

Because of these and other weaknesses of the Articles of Confederation, the founders decided to draft a new and better constitution. The very fact that they were free to change their government at any time showed the nation's potential greatness. "Happy for us," Jefferson remarked, "when we find our constitutions insufficient to secure the happiness of our people, we can assemble . . . and set it to rights, while every other nation on earth must [fight to change their systems]." [2]

Jefferson and the other American leaders met in Philadelphia on May 14, 1787. The gathering, which lasted several months, came to be called the Federal Constitutional Convention. First, the members, or **delegates**, addressed the issue of a chief executive. For ideas, they looked at historical examples. They noted, for instance, that the ancient Romans had chief administrators called consuls. But the members of Rome's legislature, the Senate, held the real power. They often used their wealth to influence the consuls' decisions. The Convention's delegates decided that the American president must be strong and independent enough to resist such influences.

A Balance of Power

This idea of making the legislature and chief executive separate and independent was not new. An English thinker named John Locke had proposed it almost a century before. The powers of the executive

Benjamin Franklin speaks to his colleagues in the 1787 Constitutional Convention.

and the legislature should be not only separate, he said, but also equal. They should balance each other. That way neither could gain too much power and impose its will on the people. Further, Locke wrote, a strong president could act quickly for the public good, especially in an emergency. By contrast, legislatures tend to act too slowly.

Thus, the delegates decided that their new government must have at least two equal branches—the president and the Congress. In addition, many delegates argued, there should be a third branch. The judges who ran the courts also held much power over the citizens. After all, a judge could

The delegates to the Constitutional Convention prepare to sign the completed Constitution. The document still had to be ratified by the states.

deprive a person of freedom by throwing him or her in jail. So the judiciary should be separate too. Those who supported this idea cited another European thinker, Frenchman Charles de Montesquieu. There can be no liberty, he wrote, "if the power of judging is not separate from legislative power and from executive power. . . . All would be lost if the same man or the same body of men . . . exercised these three powers—making laws, executing public policy, and judging crimes."[3]

Ratifying the Constitution

After much debate on these and other issues, the Convention's delegates drew up a federal constitution. It provided for three separate branches of government, including the president, Congress, and the Supreme Court. On September 17, 1787, the delegates voted to accept the document.

However, the Constitution could not take effect until at least nine of the thirteen states ratified it (gave it final approval). On June 21, 1788, New Hampshire became the ninth state to **ratify** it. On that day, the document officially took force. The remaining four states approved the Constitution between 1788 and 1790. Only a few years before, these thirteen states had been foreign colonies complaining about unfair government. Now they made up an independent nation with the fairest government in the world.

Chapter Two

Blueprint for a Democratic Government

The United States Constitution, drafted in 1787 by America's founders, is a blueprint for a fair, democratic government. It explains in clear language how the various branches of the government should work. It describes the powers held by each branch. And it shows how those powers are balanced and limited by the powers of the other branches. In addition, the Constitution provides for electing high public officials. These include the president, vice president, and members of the two houses of Congress—the Senate and House of Representatives.

People Know What Is Best for Themselves

Perhaps most important of all, in writing the Constitution the founders allowed for the concept of

The U.S. Constitution as it appeared in 1776. Its framers included a provision to allow changes (amendments) to be made.

change. They recognized that no government is perfect. Even one as good as the one they had fashioned might later be improved. Moreover, they reasoned, society and the world change over time. So there must be a way for the American people to adjust the Constitution, when necessary, to keep step with those changes. Article 5, therefore, provides for the creation of **amendments**, or changes, to the document. Under this provision, existing articles can be reworded or new articles can be added.

At the time, most people in the world looked on such ideas as strange and even dangerous. When copies of the U.S. Constitution reached Europe, most foreign leaders were shocked. To allow the people to change their government whenever they pleased was foolish, they said. It could only lead to disaster. To these leaders, most of them kings, the concept of a country run by the people was new and alien. In their view, the people of a nation are like children. The government, like a strong parent, should tell them what is best for them.

But America's founders recognized the great truth that people know what is best for themselves. As one early American leader, Virginia's John Marshall, put it, the people must be their own masters. And their leaders must be their servants: "It is the people who give power, and can take it back. What shall restrain [stop] them? They are the masters who give it, and of whom their servants [government leaders] hold it."[4]

Checks and Balances

The founders believed that the power the people gave their leaders must not be abused. This was why they provided in the Constitution for **checks** and balances among the three branches of the government. First, they gave the president a way to check the power of the Congress. When Congress passes a law, or **bill**, that law cannot become official until the president signs it. He or she can reject, or veto, the bill. Members of Congress can then rewrite the bill so that the president will accept it, or they can drop it altogether.

Most of the early presidents did not use their veto power very often. The first president, George

The Balance of Power

EXECUTIVE BRANCH

The **President of the United States** has the power to accept or reject any laws passed by Congress and to appoint Supreme Court Justices.

LEGISLATIVE BRANCH

Only **Congress** has the power to make laws and to approve or reject Supreme Court nominees.

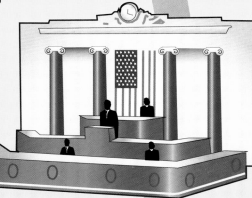

JUDICIAL BRANCH

The **Supreme Court** has the power to enforce laws and to rule that a law is illegal.

Washington, vetoed only two bills. And Thomas Jefferson, the third president, never used the veto at all. By contrast, later presidents used this power often. For example, Franklin D. Roosevelt, who served from 1933 to 1945, cast 635 vetoes!

At the same time, the Constitution allows the Congress to check the president's power. The document opens with the words, "All legislative Powers herein granted shall be vested in a Congress of the United States."[5] This means that only Congress can make laws and pass bills. The president can only accept or reject them. (He or she can *suggest* bills, but Congress does not have to accept those suggestions.) A later section of the document also gives Congress the sole power to impose taxes and to decide how the nation's money is spent.

The government's third branch, the judiciary, balances and checks both the president and Congress. If people think a new law is wrong or harmful, they can appeal to the Supreme Court. The judges, called justices, can rule that a bill passed by Congress and signed by the president is illegal under the Constitution, or unconstitutional. If so, that bill cannot become law. The founders also had the wisdom to let the president and Congress check the Supreme Court's power. No judge can make it onto the Court unless the president appoints him or her. Moreover, Congress must approve such appointments; also, Congress can remove a judge if it deems him or her unfit.

Choosing a President

The Constitution also provides for choosing the president, the single most powerful public official. According to Article 2, the president must be at least thirty-five years old. (The founders felt that a younger person would not be mature enough to make important decisions for the nation.)

Also, a president's term of office is four years. The Constitution originally allowed a president to serve an unlimited number of terms. But in the late 1940s, Congress and states changed this rule by amending the Constitution. The Twenty-second Amendment limits a president's service to two terms (or eight years). The Constitution even provides the wording of the oath the president swears

George Washington, the nation's first president, takes the oath of office.

when taking office: "I do solemnly swear (or affirm) that I will faithfully execute the Office of President of the United States, and will to the best of my Ability, preserve, protect and defend the Constitution of the United States."[6]

Electoral Versus Popular Vote

As for electing the president, Article 2 of the Constitution describes the system the founders set up for this purpose. It begins with a general election, in which all eligible citizens vote every four years. But the results of the general election do not decide who becomes president. The decision rests with the electoral college. This is not a school of higher learning. Instead, it is a group of special voters called electors. These are ordinary citizens, a few located in each state. Every four years, following the general election, the electors cast ballots to choose the president.

This process has changed a bit since the founders drafted the Constitution. Originally, the members of the state legislatures chose the electors every four years. But over time, many Americans objected. They argued that it would be fairer and more democratic if the general voters had more of a role in choosing their president. The government responded to this argument, and by 1832 all states had adopted a new system. Today the people vote to choose the electors, who then elect the president.

In the election of 2000, Republican candidate George W. Bush autographs a campaign poster (top), while his Democratic opponent, Al Gore, greets supporters (middle). Two major newspapers report the election results (bottom).

Some people feel that this system still needs improvement. In a close presidential race, they say, one candidate could win the popular vote and the other the electoral vote. The second candidate would win because the electoral vote decides the election. And he or she would become president even though a majority of Americans voted for someone else. This actually occurred in the election of 2000. Candidate Al Gore, of Tennessee, won the popular vote. However, his opponent, George W. Bush, of Texas, won the electoral vote, so Bush became president.

Although some people have called for eliminating the electoral college, others are happy with it. They say that choosing the president by direct popular vote would not be fair. According to this view, the states with the largest populations might always decide who becomes president. A few large states would then gain too much power over the others.

In any case, most people on both sides of the issue do not want to tamper with the Constitution. They admit that it is not a perfect document. But overall, they say, time has proven it to be strong, practical, and fair.

Chapter Three

The Bill of Rights Grants Basic Freedoms

When the American founders first drafted the Constitution in Philadelphia, it had no Bill of Rights. Such a bill is a list of basic freedoms such as freedom of speech, freedom of the press, and freedom of religion. This may seem strange and surprising to people today. Indeed, most Americans have come to think of the Bill of Rights *as* the Constitution, or at least the most familiar part of that document.

At first the founders did not think a Bill of Rights was needed. Their blueprint for government—the Articles of Confederation—had also lacked such a list of rights. The reason was simple. Most of the states had already passed their own local bills guaranteeing basic rights. Virginia had been the first to do so, on June 12, 1776.

The Bill of Rights, cast in bronze, is displayed in front of the Federal Building in Wilmington, Delaware.

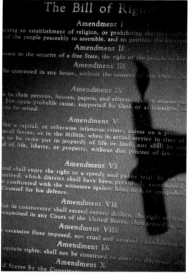

In time, however, some American leaders began to feel that these local bills of rights were not enough. The freedoms they listed differed from state to state. Also, not all states had passed such bills. In their view, the country needed a *national* bill of rights. That way, all Americans would enjoy the same, basic freedoms.

Debates over Creating a Bill of Rights

The debate over drafting a national bill of rights heated up near the end of the Constitutional Convention in 1787. George Mason, a Virginia planter and legislator, argued strongly for the bill. The Constitution should include it, he said, because "it would give great quiet [a feeling of security] to the people."[7] One of Mason's colleagues, Elbridge Gerry of Massachusetts, agreed. However, most of the other delegates disagreed and voted to approve the Constitution without a bill of rights. For this reason, Mason and Gerry refused to sign the finished Constitution.

The argument did not end there. In the months that followed, the states held their own debates about whether or not to ratify the Constitution. And one of the chief topics in these debates was a bill of rights. In Virginia, for example, Mason spoke out against accepting the Constitution as it was written. "There is no declaration of rights [in it]," he complained.

> The declarations of rights in the separate states are no security. There is no declaration of any kind [in the Constitution] for preserving the liberty of the press, the trial by jury in civil cases, nor against the danger [to everyday citizens] of standing armies in times of peace.[8]

As the debate went on, founders Thomas Jefferson and John Adams came to agree with Mason. James Madison, one of the authors of the Constitution, also changed his mind. "It is my sincere opinion," Madison said, "that the Constitution ought to be revised."[9] Supporters of a bill of rights met with opponents and worked out a compromise. Supporters

James Madison played a pivotal role in drafting the Bill of Rights.

said they would ratify the Constitution providing that such a bill was later drafted and added to the document.

Madison promptly assumed the leadership in drafting the Bill of Rights. At first he thought it best to work this list of freedoms into the Constitution's existing text. But most members of Congress favored a different approach. They felt it would be better to list each freedom as a separate amendment to the document. This view prevailed. On September 25, 1789, Congress approved the Bill of Rights and passed it on to the states for approval. The last state to ratify it was Virginia, on December 15, 1791. On that day, the bill officially became part of the U.S. Constitution.

Protecting Personal Liberties

Consisting of the first ten amendments to the Constitution, the Bill of Rights remains a cornerstone of American liberty. In fact, the bill has often been called the greatest list of human freedoms ever devised. Perhaps the most famous and often quoted is the First Amendment. The phrase "First Amendment rights" frequently comes up in the courts or in the news. These rights are the freedom to worship as one pleases; freedom of speech; freedom of the press; the right for people to assemble in groups when they so choose; and the right to demand that the government listen to people's complaints.

The other parts of the Bill of Rights are no less important in protecting personal liberties. The Second Amendment, for instance, allows people to own weapons to defend themselves. And the Fourth

Thousands of people gather in Washington, D.C., to demand that Congress pass stronger gun control laws. The Constitution's Second Amendment allows citizens to bear arms.

27

Amendment says that the police cannot search someone's house without first getting a judge's permission.

Some of the most important rights of all are guaranteed in the Sixth Amendment. These concern a person who has been accused of a crime. It declares, "the accused [once arrested] shall enjoy the right to a speedy and public trial," by a jury. The accused must "be informed of the nature and cause of the accusation [and] to be confronted with the witnesses against him."[10] The accused also has the right to be defended in court by a lawyer.

Strict Versus Loose Interpretations

To the founders, the rights guaranteed in the Bill of Rights seemed clear and straightforward. However, later generations have sometimes defined them differently. Debates about their exact meanings still go on. Some legal and political experts define these freedoms "strictly." They feel that all American citizens should enjoy them exactly as stated in the Bill of Rights, without government limits. Other experts define these freedoms "loosely." They point out that the country undergoes constant growth and changes in attitude. And the Bill of Rights must be redefined from time to time to keep pace with such growth and changes.

People often argue over the First Amendment, especially freedom of speech. Sometimes people are arrested for saying or printing something unpopular. In 1951, for example, leaders of the American Communist Party publicly argued for getting rid of democracy. Claiming this was an attempt to overthrow the government, police threw eleven of the leaders in jail. Some Americans supported this response. Sometimes free speech must be limited, they said, to protect the country and its people. Supreme Court Justice Frederick Vinson wrote: "Overthrow of the government is certainly a substantial enough interest for the government to limit free speech."[11]

But other Americans disagreed with jailing the Communist leaders. They said that this small group posed no real threat to the country or the government. They argued that the arrests overstepped the

Protesters make their views known in public. The First Amendment protects free speech, even when it is unpopular.

First Amendment. According to this view, the government cannot deprive people of freedom of speech just because it does not like what they say. That freedom, one person wrote, "holds good in war as in peace, in danger as in security." [12]

Such arguments about the meaning of the Bill of Rights continue. But all involved agree that the bill itself must never be changed. It will surely remain a guarantee of basic personal liberties for all future generations of Americans.

Chapter Four

The Constitution's Survival, Influence, and Future

For the most part, the Constitution that the founders drafted more than two centuries ago has served the United States well. By providing for a fair, open government and basic personal freedoms for all citizens, it has helped to create a nation that has served as a model for others.

Not surprisingly, this success has inspired and attracted people living elsewhere. Year after year, century after century, people from around the world have come to the United States to make new lives for themselves. Almost all have cited the same reasons—the freedom to elect their own leaders; the chance even to become one of those leaders; the freedom to go wherever they please and to express their views openly; and the opportunity to pursue their dreams. All of these are part of the great legacy that the American founders created when they crafted the Constitution.

The Nation Grows Increasingly Free

One way the Constitution made the United States a strong and important nation was by allowing it to change and grow with the times. Because the document allows for its own revision, both it and the country have improved in several ways over the years. Probably the most important improvement is that more people enjoy more freedom today than in the past. Several of the twenty-seven amendments added so far have extended freedom or protection to groups who lacked it.

When the United States was founded, for example, most black Americans were slaves. They lacked not only freedom of speech, but all other rights as well. Also, even many free Americans lacked certain basic rights. In most states, men who did not own property could not vote. And women could not vote at all, whether they owned property or not. Despite the founders' famous statement that "all men are created equal,"[13] American society was still very *un*equal.

Over the years, though, people's attitudes steadily changed. Ideas and institutions that had once seemed fair and normal came to be seen as unfair and wrong. The government repeatedly responded by amending the Constitution. And these amendments, in turn, brought about important, sometimes sweeping changes in American society.

Perhaps the most sweeping change of all was the Thirteenth Amendment, ratified in 1865. It outlaws slavery in the United States. (President Lincoln had freed the slaves in 1863, but slavery was still legal under the Constitution until approval of the Thirteenth Amendment.) The Fifteenth Amendment, ratified in 1870, says that men cannot be denied the right to vote because of race or color. At that time, women still could not vote. But this, too,

Slaves pick cotton on an American plantation. The Thirteenth Amendment outlawed slavery in the United States.

In 1863 President Abraham Lincoln shows the Emancipation Proclamation, which freed the slaves, to the members of his cabinet.

women could vote

changed when the Nineteenth Amendment gave them that right in 1920. The Twenty-sixth Amendment, ratified in 1971, gave still another group of Americans a political voice. Before that time, no one under the age of twenty-one could vote or hold public office. The amendment extends these rights to all citizens eighteen or older.

Future Changes to the Constitution?

Americans will likely seek other constitutional amendments, though not all will become law. In

March 1972, for example, Congress passed an amendment that became known as the Equal Rights Amendment, or ERA. It stated: "Equality of rights under the law shall not be denied or abridged by the United States or by any State on account of [a person's] sex."[14] This amendment was intended to do away with unequal treatment between men and women. After Congress passed it, the amendment went to the states for ratification. But too few states ratified it, so it did not become law.

Various groups and individuals would like to see other constitutional amendments become reality. Among them, for example, are many residents of

A group of women demonstrates for equal rights. Too few states ratified the Equal Rights Amendment (ERA), so it did not become law.

the District of Columbia. This is the special region occupied by Washington, D.C., the nation's capital. It is not part of any state. But a large number of people who live there would like to see it become a state, which would require amending the Constitution. Another possible amendment frequently mentioned would eliminate the electoral college. Supporters of such a change argue that it would be fairer to have the people elect the president directly, by the popular vote.

The World Transformed

The Constitution has not only proven to be the cornerstone of American democracy but also a model for the world. The South American country of Argentina,

The first three words of the U.S. Constitution—"We the People"—sum up the basic democratic principles of this document.

Visitors view original copies of the U.S. Constitution and Declaration of Independence.

for example, established a democratic constitution in 1853. It resembles the U.S. version in many ways. In particular, the Argentine constitution provides for three governmental branches—a president, Congress, and Supreme Court. The West African country of Liberia also modeled much of its constitution on that of the United States. The Philippines (in the western Pacific) did the same, along with several nations in Central America.

By 1992 the number of democratic countries in the world had grown to seventy-five. The United States had sponsored, aided, or inspired a majority of these nations. Experts predict that this trend is far from over. Many other countries, they say, will draw up democratic constitutions in the twenty-first century. Some may resemble the U.S. Constitution. Others may simply be inspired by it or by the success of the United States. Either way, one thing seems certain: The revolutionary document that transformed a nation beginning in 1787 will continue to transform the world.

Notes

Chapter One: The Founders Draft the Constitution

1. Quoted in Neal R. Pierce, *The People's President.* New York: Simon and Schuster, 1968, p. 31.
2. Quoted in Joseph J. Ellis, *American Sphinx: The Character of Thomas Jefferson.* New York: Knopf, 1997, p. 102.
3. Quoted in Diane Ravitch, ed., *Democracy Reader.* New York: HarperCollins, 1992, p. 41.

Chapter Two: Blueprint for a Democratic Government

4. Quoted in Richard Hofstadter, et al., *The United States: The History of a Republic.* Englewood Cliffs, NJ: Prentice-Hall, 1960, p. 134.
5. U.S. Constitution, Article 2, Section 1.
6. U.S. Constitution, Article 2, Section 1.

Chapter Three: The Bill of Rights Grants Basic Freedoms

7. Quoted in Catherine D. Brown, *Miracle at Philadelphia: The Story of the Constitutional Convention, May to September 1787.* Boston: Little, Brown, 1966, p. 244.

8. Quoted in J. R. Pole, ed., *The American Constitution, For and Against: The Federalist and Anti-Federalist Papers*. New York: Hill and Wang, 1987, pp. 126–27.

9. Quoted in Robert Rutland, *James Madison: Founding Father*. New York: Macmillan, 1987, p. 47.

10. U.S. Constitution, Sixth Amendment.

11. Frederick M. Vinson, majority opinion in *Dennis v. United States* (1951).

12. Alexander Meiklejohn, *Free Speech and Its Relation to Self-Government*. New York: Harper and Brothers, 1948, p. 17.

Chapter Four: The Constitution's Survival, Influence, and Future

13. Declaration of Independence.

14. Quoted in Eric Fonor and John A. Garraty, eds., *The Reader's Companion to American History*. Boston: Houghton Mifflin, 1991, p. 356.

Glossary

amendment: a change, usually made in a document

bill: A law or policy debated and/or passed by a legislature.

check: to limit the power or impact of something; or such a limit placed on someone or something

delegates: People sent by various towns, states, or organizations to attend a general meeting or convention.

executive: An administrator; the chief executive of a nation is often called a president. The executive branch of a government is the one headed by the president.

federal: national, or on the national level

judiciary: a court system, or the branch of a government that deals with legal matters

legislative: A lawmaking body made up of representatives of the people of a country. The legislative branch of a government is usually called a congress or a parliament.

ratify: to give final approval for something

For Further Exploration

Linda C. Johnson, *Our Constitution*. Brookfield, CT: Millbrook Press, 1994. An easy-to-understand overview of the document on which the United States government is based.

Brent P. Kelley, *James Madison, Father of the Constitution*. Philadelphia: Chelsea House, 2000. A well-written examination of one of the most important of the American founders.

Louise Marks and Benton Minks, *The Revolutionary War*. New York: Facts On File, 1992. Written for basic readers, this fine volume summarizes the war that gave birth to the United States and led to the drafting of the U.S. Constitution.

Don Nardo, *The Bill of Rights*. San Diego: Greenhaven Press, 1997. Consists of opposing opinions and debates about the Bill of Rights, with quotes by James Madison and the other figures who created it. A bit challenging for grade-schoolers but worth the effort.

———, *Democracy*. San Diego: Lucent Books, 1994. Traces the origins and development of democratic thought and practice, from ancient times to the writing of the U.S. Constitution, and the spread of democracy in the modern world.

Aimed at junior high readers.

———, *The Importance of Thomas Jefferson*. San Diego: Lucent Books, 1993. A concise biography of Jefferson, including his role in the formation of the infant United States. The reading level is junior high school.

Patricia R. Quiri, *The Bill of Rights*. Danbury, CT: Childrens Press, 1999. This informative book about the Bill of Rights, how it came to be, and its provisions is aimed at young readers.

———, *The Constitution*. Danbury, CT: Childrens Press, 1999. Another well-written book for young readers.

R. Conrad Stein, *The Bill of Rights*. Chicago: Childrens Press, 1992. A brief synopsis of the Bill of Rights and how it has affected American society over the years. Written for basic readers.

Index

Picture Credits

About the Author

Historian and award-winning author Don Nardo has written many books for young people about American history, including *The Mexican-American War, The Declaration of Independence, The Indian Wars,* and *Franklin D. Roosevelt: U.S. President.* Nardo lives with his wife, Christine, in Massachusetts.